Animal-Speak
Pocket
Guide

Animal-Speak Pocket Guide

by

Ted Andrews

Dragonhawk Publishing   Jackson, Tennessee

A Dragonhawk Publishing Book

Animal-Speak Pocket Guide
Copyright (c) 2009 by Ted Andrews

First Edition

Book Design by Ted Andrews
Cover Design by Ted Andrews

ISBN 978-1888767-61-2
Library of Congress Control Number:

Dragonhawk Publishing
PO Box10637
Jackson, TN 38308
USA

For Talisman -
with great love.
You are missed.

Table of Contents

"No matter how much we cloak ourselves in civilization, we will always be a part of Nature. Because of this, we should learn to listen to Her messages - especially those that come through animal brothers and sisters...

As humans, we sometimes forget that we can starve as much from a lack of wonder as we can a lack of food. When we open ourselves to animals and Nature, we open our hearts and souls to true wonders."

- Ted Andrews

Chapter One

Animal-Speak Pocket Guide

You are driving in your car and a hawk flies in front of you. The crow sitting in the tree seems to be looking right at you while strolling in the park. You dream of a lion attacking you while you are on vacation. You see yourself becoming a beautiful butterfly in your meditation. The same animal appears in every time you walk outside. A part of you knows that these encounters have meaning, but how can you truly come to understand them?

Let's be honest, as effective and insightful as my larger reference books *Animal-Speak* and *Animal-Wise* are, it is not always practical to carry them everywhere you go. You are not always in a position to discern the meaning or to study the encounter at the actual time of the encounter. And yet, you know the animal's message is important – sometimes so important that you should not wait until you get home to explore it.

The *Animal-Speak Pocket Guide* solves this problem. It is small enough to fit comfortably in a pants pocket, inside your coat, tucked easily into a purse or suitcase or into the glove compartment of your car. It provides simple keynote messages associated with more than 290 animals – including birds, mammals, insects and arachnids, reptiles and sea life. With it, you can find the basic meaning of your animal encounters wherever you go. It will provide initial guidance until you do have the time and opportunity to explore the encounter much more deeply – for more subtle nuances.

Discovering the meanings of animal messages is sometimes difficult, but there is no doubt that animal encounters – whether in dreams, waking life or meditation - stimulate some primordial part of our imagination. They help liberate the mind, opening us to possibilities beyond our daily routines.

There was a time in which humanity saw itself as part of Nature and Nature as part of it. And no matter how much we cloak ourselves in civilization today, we will always be a part of Nature. Although many have forgotten this in our modern world, animal and human are inseparable in many ways. Because of our innate connection to Nature, animals play a particularly strong role in our unconscious symbology. They are totems, allies, and messengers - providing guidance throughout our life. With the *Animal-Speak Pocket Guide*, you can now have that guidance readily at your fingertips.

Animal Messengers

Animal messengers communicate to us about our lives and about us. Discovering the meanings of the messages they bring is sometimes difficult, but there is no doubt that animal encounters – whether in dreams or waking life, stimulate some primordial part of our imagination. Using this pocket guide will help you liberate the mind - opening you to greater possibilities within your daily routines.

There are five main types of animal totems and messengers that we are all likely to have in our life. There is some variation depending upon the particular tradition, and some of the roles overlap. For example, a power animal may also be a protector and a message bringer. We can also have several animals in each of these categories.

Message Bringers

All animals in Nature are message bringers. Their appearance provides guidance in our life. They bring direction to us about situations, choices, decisions and activities we are involved in. A closer study of their characteristics and behaviors provide clues and insight as to what our behaviors and actions should be in situations around us. When we have a problem, asking for guidance and then taking a nature walk to get the message is one of the best ways of finding answers.

Personal Power Animals

Power totems are animals that are with us throughout our life or through major periods within our life. They are message bringers, protectors, teachers and healers. Different traditions disagree about how many power animals we have. It can vary, each animal working and helping us in different areas of our life.

For example, one of my totems is the red-tailed hawk. I have worked hands on with hawks and other birds of prey for many years, but I have also worked spiritually with them for many years.

Hawk has helped me to develop and focus my spiritual / psychic vision. It has taught me patience and it serves as a messenger to warn me of the ease or difficulty of the path ahead of me. But it is not my only power animal. If the same animal appears repeatedly over a longer period of time (more than a year), it is likely one of you power animals.

Protectors

Protectors are often power animals, but these are animals that give us extra strength and energy, often without our realizing it at the moment. They alert us to trouble. They often appear in dreams of conflict to let us know what qualities to draw on to handle the conflicts in our life. Many people wrongly assume that protectors are always big and ferocious animals. They can be, but every animal has its own unique defense strategies and abilities. While bears can be powerful protectors for many aspects life, the opossum can also serves as a protector, warning that things and people around us are not what they seem to be. We may need to "play possum" in some situations. Remember that every animal has its own unique way of protecting itself and defending its home.

Teacher

All animals that come to us are teachers. They teach us about our own potentials, about energies at play within our life and about our spiritual path in this life. We can learn something from every animal, but those who appear regularly have something special to teach us, something we need to learn. Pay attention to animals that appear regularly while using the oracle.

Animals also serve as spiritual guides for us, leading us and helping us in sacred quests and journeys and so the oracle can help you with this as well. Often animals that appear regularly in our dreams are teaching totems. They are guides into and out of the dream world and the underworld. This pocket guide can be used for all kinds of insight and teaching for every aspect of our life.

Healing

The pocket guide will also help find animal totems that can provide you with energy and guidance in regards to healing others or yourself. Many animals have unique resistance to certain diseases and drawing upon that animal's energy helps us be more resistant to it as well. Some animals are archetypal symbols of healing. The snake is one such animal. It sheds the old skin and moves into the new. It is a symbol of leaving the old behind for the new. As a symbol of transformation, meditating and focusing on the snake during times of illness will help accelerate the healing process. Animals that appear to us at times of illness provide clues as to the best way to focus our healing energies.

The Animal-Speak Pocket Guide

Throughout the world, people have always looked to Nature for healing, spiritual guidance, omens and messages and each of us can learn to read and understand those communications. Often though, we have encounters or experiences when we are unable to study and explore their significance at that time.

Now you no longer have to wait to uncover the meaning of an animal encounter. The *Animal-Speak Pocket Guide* can travel with you. You can begin your understanding and can get guidance wherever you are.

What am I supposed to do in life? How do I really know what choice to make? Where are things headed for me? What have I set in motion? Imagine if we could get answers to our most important questions. Imagine if we had signposts to guide us. Well, the truth is that we do not have to go through life blindly. In the realm of Nature, there are a myriad of signposts to guide, direct and answer our questions.

Drawing upon decades of work with wildlife, along with a lifetime study of things mystical, I have created this pocket guide as a portable companion to my larger books on animals and their messages. It will help guide you in your life. Clear and insightful, this pocket guide will help you recognize and understand communications of the animal world wherever you are. It will offer an epiphany for your heart and guidance for the soul. You will find quick answers and initial direction.

Animals are our companions, allies, teachers, guardians, and message bringers. Through The *Animal-Speak Pocket Guide*, these roles will crystallize for you and the animals will become powerful signposts - bridges to the phenomenal world of spirit – wherever you are throughout the day.

Chapter Two

Birds

Birds in myths and tales are often symbols of the soul. Their ability to fly reflects our ability to rise to new awareness. They reflect the ability to link the physical realms with those of the sky (heavens). Because of this, they are the most frequent messengers of spirits and angels.

Birds link the waking with the dreaming. We are all given to flights of fancy, a phrase often used to describe our dreams and imaginations. As totems and spirit animals, each bird has its own peculiar characteristics, but they all can be aids for inspiration, hope and new ideas.

Albatross *(alert for signs)*
Be alert for signs of approaching opportunities. Commit to opportunities fully if you wish to find success.

Barred Owl   *(gentle intuition)*
Spirits are calling. Pay attention to all of the signs. Although small, subtle and quiet, heed that gentle voice of your intuition.

Bittern   *(face problems)*
More is going on than is apparent, so do not ignore the signs. When you face the troubles, the answers will appear.

Blackbird   *(protect what's yours)*
Usually a good sign of promise, it is important to stake out your territory. The forces of Nature are with you now.

Blackbird - Red winged   *(surprises)*
New surprises and understanding are coming. Your efforts will be noticed. Secrets revealed that give new perspective.

Bluebird   *(happiness)*
Gentleness brings happiness. Do not force transitions. Allow change to come in the manner best for you.

Blue Jay   *(choose wisely)*
Be careful of choices you make. Choose so others do not get hurt. Don't be afraid. Stay with choices you have made.

Bob White   *(protect secrets)*
It is time to protect your secrets. Do not let others know your plans or ideas. All eyes are on you, but there is strength through silence.

Burrowing Owl   *(underworld)*
Stay grounded while working with spirits. Underworld may be opening for you. Keep your sense of humor.

Canary   *(power of voice)*
Trust in the power of your voice. It can powerfully influence   others - hurt or heal. Work with music brings joy.

Caracara   *(adaptability)*
Use the available resources. Be adaptable in all things. Facial expressions will reveal much about you and others.

Cardinal   *(renewed importance)*
Accept you life's importance. Accept yourself as a source of light and do not be afraid to conduct yourself accordingly.

Catbird   *(communication)*
Be careful of how you communicate. Explore new ways of expressing and relating to others. Your words have greater power.

Chickadee   *(truth revealed)*
Discover and express the truth. Lies and deceptions will be found out. Threats will pass. Show no fear. Truth will out.

Chicken   *(fertility & divination)*
This is a time of fertility in most areas of your life. Explore forms of divination to determine where best to place efforts.

Cockatoo   *(focus on relationships)*
Strengthen your relationship bonds – marital, personal and business. Good time to court new favors in love and business.

Condor   *(ancient spirits)*
Time of great protection and spirit contact surrounds you. You will soon soar above previous limitations.

Conure   *(attend to family)*
Attend to the family and young around you. They require attention and careful expression. Choose words carefully.

Cormorant   *(dive deeper)*
Dive deeper for answers and solutions. Trust in your methods. You will accomplish things now in unique ways what others can not.

Cowbird   *(family issues)*
Resolve family relationships and problems, Parent and child issues come to forefront. Good time to resolve issues.

Crane   *(guardianship)*
Spiritual justice is at play. Karma will be playing out somewhere in your life. Reflect on past lives and past issues.

Crow   *(magical help)*
Unexpected help with problems and obstacles is at hand to bring relief. Your magic is calling and it will be answered.

Cuckoo   *(new fate)*
A new fate is unfolding and calling. A new spring is upon you. Trust in the new fate that you have sought for some time.

Dove   *(peace)*
A new cycle of opportunities is at hand. They bring a time of peace and prophecy. Mourn and release what has passed for new birth.

Duck   *(emotions soothed)*
Seek out emotional comfort and protection. Stay in comfortable environment. Difficulties will be easily handled.

Eagle *(healing visions)*
Spirit Vision and healing surround you. Look at things from new perspective. Take a different path. Trust what you are becoming.

Emu *(responsibility)*
Fulfill responsibilities while you explore possibilities. Follow your wandering spirit but do not neglect your responsibilities.

Falcon *(act swiftly)*
Take action when opportunity appears. Quick maneuvers will succeed and impress others. You will stir respect in others.

Finch *(increased activity)*
Activity increases around you. Greater opportunities are at hand. They will not be lost, so just do what you can.

Flamingo *(healing)*
Now is the time to heal the heart. Follow your heart in all endeavors. Seek out what heals and nourishes the heart.

Flicker *(new starts)*
New beginnings are near. There is an opportunity for new growth. Trust in your ability to manifest healing love.

Goldfinch   *(nature spirits)*
Increased contact with spirits of nature abound.
Listen and communicate on all levels as inner and
outer realms open to you.

Goose   *(follow quest)*
Heed the call to the new quest. Open to new wonders and possibilities. Pursue new adventures.
Explore new travels.

Goshawk   *(skillful pursuit)*
If you can dream it, you can achieve it. Focus on
what is plentiful and seek out a variety of nourishments for your soul.

Grackle   *(handle emotions)*
Free the emotions and anxieties. They have locked
everything into limbo. Seek out help and advice
to uncomplicated your life.

Great Blue Heron   *(be assertive)*
(See heron.) Assert your authority and strike while
you can. Trust in your jack-of-all-trades abilities
but be careful of dabbling.

Grebe   *(creative environments)*
You need a more creative environment. Seek out
and dive into creative waters. Pay attention to
dream activity.

Grosbeak   *(healing of the heart)*
Take new pride and a sense of nobility in the parenting process. Now is the time to focus on family and sing a new healing melody.

Grouse   *(sacred dance)*
A time of new sacred rhythms is at hand. A new dance will work best for you now. Change your routines and the sacred will manifest.

Gyrfalcon   *(sacred gift)*
Maintain a knightly code in your activities. A sacred gift is coming. Efforts will be rewarded. Slow and steady wins.

Harrier Hawk   *(spirit messages)*
Stay grounded while maneuvering among new spirit and psychic energies. Take care of daily obligations.

Harris Hawk   *(cooperation)*
Trust in your vision but also trust in others' abilities to help you accomplish goals. Cooperate with others for greater success.

Hawk   *(guiding vision)*
Spirit vision and guardianship surround you. Be patient and observe. You will see the opportunities. Signs are clear.

Heron *(be assertive)*
Assert yourself when opportunities appear.
Change is coming anyway so act with self-reliance.
Take advantage of changes.

Hummingbird *(renewal)*
Dreams and new joy are within reach -opportunity
for accomplishment, along with promising success
and renewed health.

Ibis *(healing and magic)*
Healing, magic and protection surround you.
Take on opportunities to learn new healing and
magical arts.

Junco *(replenishment)*
New waters are coming that will replenish you.
Opportunities for new growth will occur soon.
Facial expressions reveal much.

Kestrel *(agility)*
Act with speed and grace. Trust in your mental
agility to succeed. Now is the time to commit fully
to your actions.

Killdeer *(protect your creations)*
Guard your creative activities and artistic endeavors now. Do not expose them too quickly to the
outer world and its threats.

Kingfisher *(new sunshine)*
New sunshine, prosperity and love are coming. Have faith in yourself and your abilities. Winter is finally passing.

Kite *(adapt)*
You need to be adaptable and flexible now. Use the skills that you have available to you. New skills learned more easily.

Lark *(harmony and luck)*
Your own sacred song is being awakened. The mysteries of sound and music should be developed and used.

Long-Eared Owl *(silent defense)*
Nighttime will be more productive and creative for you. Be silent but assertive in your endeavors. Protect activities.

Loon *(prophetic dreams)*
Pay attention to the important dream activity now. Opportunities to fulfill hopes, wishes and dreams are at hand.

Macaw *(trust perceptions)*
Trust your sharp vision and spirit perception, especially in regards to health issues. Trust perceptions, no matter how strange.

Magpie   *(secrets revealed)*
Secrets are being uncovered and discovered. Use this knowledge properly. Benefits are coming but in an unusual and unexpected manner.

Martin   *(change of fortune)*
This is a time of good luck or a change in your fortune. Peaceful living energies are building. Moves will be positive.

Meadowlark   *(cheerful Journey)*
Find joy within yourself rather than outside of you. Every event is part of a greater journey. Find joy in the seeking and the journey.

Merlin   *(quick shapeshifting)*
The time for magical maneuverings is at hand. Be cautious of others. Shapeshifting and illusion helps accomplish goals.

Mockingbird   *(awaken abilities)*
Look for new opportunities on your path to sing forth your own song. Awaken and express your abilities. Do not hold back.

Night Hawk   *(diligence)*
(See swisher.) Be diligent and persist in your endeavors. Nothing succeeds like persistence. Half-hearted efforts fail.

Nuthatch *(faith)*

Have faith but not blind faith in others. Free yourself of preconceptions. Faith in you leads to strength and proper action.

Oriole *(weaving the new)*

New sunshine is coming. Explore the inner child and seek a renewed sense of joy in life. Prayer is more effective now.

Osprey *(assertive hunting)*

Assert new efforts. Check your commitments to others and theirs to you. Now is time for active and fearless hunting.

Ostrich *(be grounded)*

Be practical and grounded with the new knowledge coming to you. Assimilate knowledge before acting on it.

Owl *(spirits)*

(See individual owls.) Spirits are strong around you. Attend to dreams and to heightened senses. It is up to you to act on that guidance.

Parakeet *(messenger companion)*

New spirit guide is at hand. You may need to look for new associates or you may need to just spend some time alone.

Parrot   *(diplomacy)*
Develop and use power of speech for success. Be diplomatic in your activities. New understanding of others is coming.

Peacock   *(resurrection)*
Protection comes now through psychic and clairvoyant perceptions. Rebirth and resurrection will happen.

Pelican   *(unselfishness)*
Unselfishness will renew you. Give what you can to others. You will not be overcome by current situations.

Penguin   *(follow dreams)*
Trust in your dream. Now is the time to make it a reality. Use your creativity and imagination. Now is the time to act.

Peregrine Falcon   *(power and speed)*
Do not hesitate to act swiftly when opportunity appears. Dive quickly and pursue with greatest speed wherever it takes you.

Pheasant   *(fertile time)*
This is a time of fertility, creativity and success. Pursue your ideas. Explore and express your creativity for rewards.

Pigeon   *(return home)*

Seek security around and in the home. If storms arise, huddle with your family – biological or otherwise.

Puffin   *(prayer and humor)*

Prayer and a sense of humor will get you through most things in life. Don't take spiritual so seriously. Work, pray and have fun.

Quail   *(group protection)*

Protection and success comes best through groups. Be mindful of dangers. Do not hesitate in crises and explode to safety if threatened.

Raven   *(shapeshifting)*

Things are shapeshifting around you. There is an awakening of magic. Give it new expression and life will change for the better.

Roadrunner   *(mental agility)*

Stimulate the mind but do not over think. Ideas are flowing. Act quickly upon them. You need to think quickly on your feet.

Robin   *(spring at hand)*

A new spring is upon you. Trust in your new creative ideas. Stretch yourself into new areas. Your efforts will be rewarded.

Rooster   *(fertility)*

Time of increased fertility and resurrection is at hand. Optimism increases. Sexuality grows stronger.

Sandhill Crane   *(sacred guard)*

Secret and noble guardianship surrounds you. You may need to protect another. It is time to participate in the dance of life.

Sapsucker   *(hidden sweetness)*

Seek out sweetness beneath the surface. Find nourishment and resources that are around you. Hidden nectar is coming your way.

Sea Gull   *(behave)*

Adjust your behavior and how you communicate. Do not force or argue your way into anything new for success.

Secretary Bird   *(follow heart)*

Use what you have & do what is best for you. Stand tall in your uniqueness., but maintain proper behavior and customs.

Sharp-Shinned Hawk   *(timing)*

Be prepared to act when opportunity appears. Trust in your sense of timing. You will maneuver around obstacles with ease.

Short-Eared Owl   *(pursue aggressively)*
Carefully develop and use your life skills consciously. Be meticulous in details but pursue your goals strongly.

Sparrow   *(nobility)*
Trust in your nobility. Fulfill responsibilities. Pursue and do what you need to do for yourself. Obstacles soon will pass out of view.

Starling   *(etiquette)*
Proper behavior and communication will benefit you now – especially in group situations. Be careful of what you say and how you say it.

Stork   *(birth)*
Focus your movements for best success. To transcend present conditions and open to new birth, exert your efforts more clearly.

Swallow   *(proper perspective)*
Keep a proper perspective now. Be objective and distance yourself from problems. It will protect you and your environment.

Swan   *(magical wonders)*
Magical realms are opening. Trust in your heart, your true self and your creativity. New opportunities are coming.

Swift *(pursue)*

Act now in pursuit of your quest. Take advantage of opportunities. Rely on yourself and draw upon the magical waters within.

Swisher *(persistence)*

(See night hawk) Persistence is the key to accomplishment now. Do not neglect the little things. Inspiration comes at dawn and dusk.

Tufted Titmouse *(dignity)*

Maintain your dignity and your inner nobility. Little things count and serve a great function. Fulfill responsibilities.

Turkey *(blessings)*

Blessings and abundance are present. Your efforts will soon be rewarded. Rewards will be proportionate to your efforts.

Vulture – Black *(fulfillment)*

Time of transformation is approaching. Do not resist it. It will ultimately be to your benefit in spite of contrary appearances.

Vulture - Turkey *(rebirth)*

A time of rebirth and renewed health is at hand. This is a time of endings and beginning. Trust that process to be for your benefit.

Waxwing   *(sharing)*
Gentleness and sharing are important now. Courtesy is critical to success. Develop a new perspective of yourself.

White Crane   *(karmic justice)*
Spiritual justice will play out in the mundane world. It will unfold in the time, manner and means best for you.

Woodcock   *(be circumspect)*
Watch everything around you. What was hidden becomes visible. Opportunity can come from any direction. Be prepared.

Woodpecker   *(new rhythm)*
Time of new rhythms and new beginnings is here. Build for the future in the manner best for you alone for success.

Wren   *(resourceful)*
Be resourceful and bold, using what is available to you. Confront obstacles and resistance. Keep your eye on the big picture.

Bird Notes

Bird Notes

Chapter Three

Insects & Arachnids

Insects and arachnids are powerful parts of nature. They make powerful totems and spirit animals with ancient mythological histories. Most people look upon insects as pests, but they serve a powerful purpose in the chain of life. They each have unique qualities, reflecting archetypal influences with which we can align. Metamorphosis is the most common aspect associated with all insects and many arachnids. These messengers tell us something about the changes that are going on around us or inside of us.

Ant   (*industriousness*)
Pursue your work for the common good. If your efforts are true, the rewards will follow. Build from the ground up –no short cuts.

Insects & Arachnids

Bee *(fertility)*
This is a time of fertility and strong sexuality. Extract honey while the sun shines. Be creative in as many ways possible.

Beetle *(resurrection)*
Resurrection and change are necessary now. Leave the past behind and be protective of changes you initiate.

Black & Yellow Argiope *(new realms)*
Look for new perspectives. New dimensions are opening. You may be missing conspicuous oppotunity to explore new realms.

Black Widow Spider *(change of fate)*
New fate is being woven. The chemistry of your body or your life is changing. Keep creations in the dark until ready to shine.

Brown Spider *(slow healing)*
Examine close personal relationships. Deal with hidden hurts and betrayals from the past. Time will help heal.

Butterfly *(new birth)*
New love and joy are coming. Transformation is inevitable but will be easier than expected. Embrace the new beginnings.

Caterpillar *(good luck)*

Good luck and new birth are at hand. Take a gentle and quiet approach to endeavors. Be realistic and shed the old.

Centipede *(psychic protection)*

Stay alert to pitfalls in relationships. You are protected as you explore. Be careful of deceptions and deceiving.

Cicada *(past)*

Happiness from your past is returning. Surprising gift or offering will touch your heart. Explore past life connections.

Cockroach *(adaptability)*

Be adaptable and sensitive to subtle changes. Adaptability essential in all environments now. Be flexible and adapt to outside pressures.

Cricket *(belief)*

Power of your beliefs is strong – for good or bad. Do not distort ideas. Trust your own intuition before believing others.

Daddy Longlegs *(relationships)*

(spider variety) It is time to weave a deeper relationship. New balance in old relationships may be necessary. Initiate resolutions.

Insects & Arachnids

Dragonfly   *(time to shine)*
Trust in the power of your light and your perceptions to succeed. Efforts are maturing. Spiritual path is ahead.

Damselfly   *(shine and heal)*
Your intuition and perceptions are clear now. You are entering a new stage on your path. Step forward, Illumine and heal.

Earthworm   *(work old ground)*
Work through things carefully. Cast off what is not beneficial. Do not put self in vulnerable position. Face realities for new growth.

Firefly   *(inspiration)*
Keep your hope strong. New inspiration is awakening. Trust your own rhythms. Hope is critical to fulfillment and accomplishment.

Flea   *(irritations)*
Irritations and aggravations will increase until necessary change is made. Do not ignore problems. Assert yourself.

Fly   *(deal with issues)*
Issues of the past few weeks are growing more troublesome. Tend to responsibilities. Look to subtle clues for solutions.

Grasshopper   *(make leaps)*
Have faith. New leaps of happiness are coming.
Listening to your own inner voice brings success.
Refusing to move creates problems.

Jumping Spider   *(safe to leap)*
Now is a safe time to leap upon new opportunities.
Stretch your creative boundaries. There is safety
in exploring now.

Ladybug   *(wish fulfilled)*
Wish will be fulfilled soon. Do not push too hard
or it will be delayed. Allow efforts to unfold and
manifest in the time best for us.

Leech   *(allow healing)*
This is time to cleanse and allow joy to flow in
your life. Thin out the clutter of your life so joy
and healing can occur more naturally.

Luna Moth   *(protection & success)*
(See silkworm moth.) Greater protection exists
now in all endeavors. This is a time of abundance
and success. Face inhibitions.

Millipede   *(psychic sensitivity)*
New psychic energies and environments are
opening. Psychic sensitivity increases; clairvoyant
dreams strong.

Mosquito *(self worth)*

Protect yourself against attacks on your self-worth. Irritations and unsolved issues become aggravating. Focus on personal joys.

Moth *(sexuality)*

New relationship & sexual energies/activities are strong now. People respond strongly. Trust what smells right to you.

Orb Weaver Spider *(creative designs)*

Begin to weave and engineer your creative ideas. Now is the time to capture what you need. Eliminate what you no longer need.

Praying Mantis *(stillness)*

Be patient for success. Be alert to opportunities and to dangers. Develop stillness and trust in your intuitive abilities.

Scorpion *(transformation)*

Now is the time for transformation. Passions increase. Changes can be calm or chaotic – depending upon your self-control.

Silkworm Moth *(fertility)*

Enjoy a time of success and fulfillment. Do not be inhibited by change. Express joy, hope and renewed efforts.

Slug *(move to the light)*
No shortcuts exist now. Illumination is at hand. Appearances are deceiving but you have found your path. Let others think what they will.

Snail *(vulnerable)*
Protect your vulnerable emotions and spirit. Bring your Holy Inner Child out of the shell. Look at walls you have built around you.

Spider *(weaving fate)*
(See individual species.) Don't take the round about way – be straight. Weave something new. Trust feeling rather than seeing.

Stick Bug *(activity beneath surface)*
Be patient. There is activity beneath the surface. Continue to protect your endeavors quietly. Deal with issues of distrust.

Tarantula *(heightened psychism)*
Change and success come now through greater psychic sensitivity and trusting your own feelings. Distract threats and irritations.

Tick *(unbalanced relationship)*
Relationship(s) is unbalanced. Others may be taking advantage. Examine what is affecting your own vitality and joy.

Insects & Arachnids

Wasp *(protection)*

Protection is strong around you. Dreams are fulfilled through practical efforts and fulfilling your role and responsibilities.

Water Spider *(lucid dreaming)*

Pay attention to your dreams. They are increasingly prophetic. You can adapt successfully to environments that seem alien.

Wolf Spider *(pursue)*

Assert and pursue your opportunities more aggressively. Keep your endeavors close to you until ready to hatch. They need protecting.

Woolly Caterpillar *(change of climate)*

Change of climate is coming. Trust in their benefits. Projects do best in fall or in spring. Other times will be premature and fruitless.

Insect & Arachnid Notes

Insect & Arachnid Notes

Chapter Four

Mammals

Syymbols of fertility and creativity, mammals are distinguished from other animals primarily by the feeding of the young with milk from the mother's body. Mammals are all warm-blooded, and with the exception of a few whales, they all have a certain amount of hair or fur. They help us in staying grounded and with the practical aspects of life. They are frequently the keys to accomplishing life goals and for guiding us to our true potentials within life. Like the milk they feed their young, they remind us that the Earth provides the nourishment we require.

Aardvark *(unearth hidden)*
Your answers lie beneath the surface. If you continue to dig, answers will be found. Trust what smells right to you.

Antelope *(quick thinking)*
Be on your toes. Quick thinking required to avoid problems and to gain success. Be flexible, find essence in parched experiences.

Ape *(communication)*
Be creative in your communications and expressions. Now is time for open communication and honest expressions.

Arctic Fox *(seasonal change)*
Changes are coming with the change of seasons. Camouflage new activities. Prepare what you need to survive changes easily.

Armadillo *(self-protection)*
Sensitivity and susceptibility to outside influences are increasing, so use discrimination and protect yourself.

Ass (donkey) *(humility)*
Be wise but humble in new opportunity. People are noticing you, so you do not need to promote yourself. Stubbornness can hinder.

Baboon *(sacred space)*
Maintain groundedness and your sacred space. Do not allow yourself or your ideas to be intruded upon. Keep issues in the family.

Badger   *(self-reliance)*

Dig beneath the surface for answers and trust in your self-reliance. Learn to be comfortable with yourself and your manner of self-expression.

Bat   *(initiation)*

It is a time for change and for a new beginning. An initiation is at hand. Trust your instincts and look for hidden implications around you.

Bear   *(inner voice)*

Inner potentials are awakening. Trust your own unique rhythms - not those of others. This will bring the honey you seek.

Beaver   *(build)*

Build toward your dreams. Do not neglect what is most important to you. Now is the time for action not daydreaming.

Beluga   *(creative spirit)*

Great creativity and new dimensions are opening. The spirit of your creative waters is strong. New spiritual healing path is opening.

Bison   *(abundance)*

Abundance awaits if you act with respect and honor. Now is the time for right action. Short cuts and ingratitude create problems.

Boar   *(fidelity)*

Draw on the family strength and fidelity. Protect what you call your family. Hold true to your faith to maneuver through congestion.

Bobcat   *(silent secrets)*

Strength and success comes through silence. Do not let others know of your intentions. New knowledge is coming. Make up your own mind.

Bull   *(fertility)*

Fertile time approaches if you are not too stubborn. Sew new seeds and do now rush them to grow. Work to make life fertile.

Camel   *(successful survival)*

Survival is promised through your difficult journeys. Replenish yourself. Stay positive and the difficult will pass.

Capybara   *(seek refuge)*

Find refuge in spiritual activities. Seek out comfortable emotional, creative and spiritual waters. There is safety in the familiar.

Caribou   *(migration)*

Movement and travel are necessary now. Success comes through making moves with others. This is not a time to be idle.

Cat   *(independence)*
Mystery and magic is afoot, but you must find your own way of expressing it. Develop your ability to be more independent.

Cheetah   *(act quickly)*
Act with speed and flexibility. Be ready to maneuver and pursue opportunities when they appear. Now is time for all out efforts.

Chimpanzee   *(use tools)*
Be innovative and use new tools to accomplish tasks. Now is a time to reflect on your life and explore new life strategies for path ahead.

Chipmunk   *(balance work)*
Balance work and play to enjoy treasures of the earth. Keep creations protected and out of sight. Trust what you hear in others' voices.

Cougar   *(come into power)*
You are coming into your power. Assert yourself in all things but do not become aggressive. Take charge and be decisive.

Cow   *(nourishment)*
This is a time of fertility and new birth. Nourish yourself and others. Be as productive as you can be.

Coyote   *(wisdom & folly)*
Balance work and fun in your new endeavors. Trust that all is happening according to plan. Do what is best – even if it is difficult.

Deer   *(lure to adventures)*
Move gently into new areas. Follow the lure to new studies. Practical pursuits bring surprising rewards.

Dingo   *(relentless)*
Be relentless in order to succeed. Persistence will often win out over talent. Do not be overly cautious once decision is made.

Dog   *(faithfulness)*
Be faithful and alert to protect endeavors and those closest to you. Look at your companionship as it relates to your success.

Dolphin   *(new promise)*
Use the creative power of communication for best success. New growth is promised if you pursue new methods.

Eland   *(spirit warnings)*
Pay attention. Divine spirit messages and warnings are about. Be alert to changes in your environment.

Elephant *(traditional power)*
Past life knowledge and ancient power is awakening. Respect traditions – your own and others. Act on what is best for all.

Elk *(strength & stamina)*
Do what must be done. Strength and stamina are key to your success. Do not give up. You don't have to handle tasks alone.

Fawn *(rediscover innocence)*
Step out slowly into new endeavors. Explore with fresh innocence. New wonders are about to appear. Maintain a fresh outlook.

Ferret *(stealth)*
New agility in protecting and uncovering secrets is at hand. Don't be afraid to explore; secrets will be uncovered. Balance ferocity and play.

Fox *(magic afoot)*
Situations are shifting; magic is afoot. Do not reveal too much of your plans. Look to what might be camouflaged around you.

Gazelle *(respond quickly)*
Trust your intuition and act quickly to avoid trouble and complications. You can achieve where others would fail.

Mammals

Gibbon   *(extend your reach)*

Take on new projects. Leap for new areas of possibility. Do not let unreasonable fear hinder you. Maintain close family ties. .

Giraffe   *(farsightedness)*

Look ahead; be alert to what is coming. You can see what others cannot. Do not resist moving into new areas.

Goat   *(surefootedness)*

Seek new heights but be careful of steps. Be careful of becoming too serious in your pursuits. No need to rush right now.

Gorilla   *(gentle nobility)*

Trust in your inner strength and nobility. Focus on the care of others for your greatest success. Take pride in handling responsibilities.

Guinea Pig   *(communing & healing)*

Join with others of like mind for great healing work. Explore new possibilities and new sacred rites. Find people who believe as you do.

Hamster   *(preparation)*

Study and explore what arouses your curiosity. Make preparations for the future. Explore many creative endeavors for success.

Hedgehog   (curiosity)
Inquisitiveness brings surprises. Though misunderstood, do not hide away. Explore but protect yourself while doing so.

Hippopotamus   (baptism)
Act on your creative ideas; sacred energies are awakening. Do not let others distract. Immerse yourself into the spiritual and the healing.

Horse   (movement)
Continue forward in your efforts with discipline. New journeys are ahead. Stretch your freedom and power.

Humpback Whale   (new birth)
New birth is coming to your life. You can create through song and sound. Initial endeavors may be difficult, but greater strength soon follows.

Hyena   (be formidable)
Instincts are strong now – trust and act on them. Find a clan to support you. Communications are empowered – for good or bad.

Impala   (new leaps)
Do not hesitate to make new leaps. Listen to what others do not say. Success comes more gracefully than you imagine possible.

Jackal *(guardianship)*

Guidance and protection in new realms and endeavors are strong now. Psychic perceptions alert to adversity or to new opportunity.

Jaguar *(reclaim)*

Now is the time to reclaim the fruits of your labors. With discipline, the rewards will surprise. Patience and silence is important.

Kangaroo *(no backtracking)*

Move forward - not back. There is strength in you to overcome problems. Continue forward once you start or you will be tripped up.

Koala *(relief)*

Calm down, relax and detoxify your life. Relief comes if you allow it. Watch becoming overly emotional. Rise above shortcomings of others.

Lemur *(spirit contact)*

Clairaudience and spirit contact increasing. The signs are clear. Take time to open to their communications or you will feel haunted.

Lion *(strength of will)*

Intuition is working. Now is time for strength of will, patience and creative imagination. Do not force anything.

Llama   *(surefootedness)*

Balance stubbornness and caution in new endeavors. Climb slowly in your endeavors. Make sure you are on solid ground.

Lynx   *(hidden revealed)*

Trust in what you see and feel might be hidden. Perceptions are amazingly strong. Keep confidences and secrets to avoid problems.

Manatee   *(trust)*

Trust in what your hearts knows is right. Then pursue goals. Examine your trust in others and follow your sense of righteousness.

Mole   *(make your luck)*

Luck in endeavors comes now through your own efforts. Treasures you have been seeking are close – continue efforts.

Moose   *(new power)*

New birth of power is coming. Invitation to deepen awareness approaches. A unique and sacred energy is being awakened.

Mouse   *(details)*

Focus on the details;. Attend to the little things will lead to bigger opportunities. Do not allow your attention to be distracted.

Musk Ox   *(protection)*

Protection comes best in groups. Draw on ancient and primal strength to protect what is yours. Find the strength within.

Muskrat   *(maneuver)*

Maneuver through your emotions and the new spiritual waters. Don't trust what you see; but what subtly sounds and smells right.

Opossum   *(appearances)*

Be careful of appearances. Divert attention away from important endeavors. Pose as you must to succeed.

Orangutan   *(cleverness)*

Find new & clever uses for what is available. Put your best face forward. Changing faces and environments around you become clearer.

Orca   *(creative depths)*

Seek out new depths and new sources for creative nourishment. Working with others opens new opportunities.

Otter   *(use skills)*

Others recognize your skills. Use your creativity and your skills in new ways. Make sure you can work and have fun at the same time.

Panda Bear   *(sensitivity)*
Combine gentleness with strength for success. A quiet unassuming presence brings success. Focus and follow efforts through to completion.

Panther   *(reclaim)*
Reclaim what is rightfully yours. What has been stolen, lost or broken will be replaced by something more beneficial.

Polar Bear   *(supernatural)*
Great teachings and supernatural power is at hand. Veils are opening. Spiritual initiation is upon you. Look for new wonders.

Porcupine   *(renewed wonder)*
Balance work and play. Keep your sense of wonder alive. Resist the barbs of others. Protect your inner child.

Prairie Dog   *(community)*
Examine your social activity and community involvement. Share in responsibilities and work. Involve yourself in spite of others.

Rabbit   *(wait)*
Look for fertile signs and use the lunar cycle. If unsure, wait. Answers will become clear within a month. Then movement is assured.

Raccoon   *(disguise)*
Transformation comes through putting on a proper mask. Masking is going on – for good or for bad. Disguising intentions may be necessary.

Ram   *(new beginnings)*
Make necessary sacrifices for successful new beginnings. Initiate – don't think – about new endeavors. Take advantage of small openings.

Rat   *(industrious)*
Be resourceful and shrewd for greatest success. Explore as many new avenues as possible. Do not limit your activities or efforts.

Rhinoceros   *(ancient wisdom)*
Put your life in perspective and trust your own wisdom. Be more discriminating. Do not distrust the foundation you have laid.

Sea Lion   *(imagination)*
Apply your imagination to your work. Others' ideas are not always better. Balance imagination with practical application.

Seal   *(dream activity)*
Trust in your dreams and explore your creativity. Dreams become lucid and prophetic. Do not become lost in them.

Shrew   *(vision in the dark)*

Watch energy levels and prepare for tougher times. You will see your way through the dark in spite of outside circumstances.

Siberian Tiger   *(passion)*

Expect an expansion of your power and sensibilities. Control your passions. Do not let them become unpredictable.

Skunk   *(boundaries)*

Now is the time to assert your boundaries. Others may be taking advantage. Demand respect and move forward at your speed.

Snow Leopard   *(face fears)*

Opportunity arises to face your fears and demons with success. New vistas open by dealing with obstacles.

Squirrel   *(work and play)*

Balance your work and play. Prepare for the future, but do not get lost in preparations. Find ways to gather and to gift.

Tiger   *(power)*

(See Siberian Tiger.) Assert your power in new endeavors. New adventures will bring opportunity to express power and passion.

Walrus　　　　　*(psychic touch)*
Powerful psychic touch is awakening. Opportunity to uncover the hidden arises. Trust what you feel, in spite of outer appearances.

Weasel　　　　　*(secrets)*
Be observant. Secrets will be revealed and trouble circumvented by doing so. Do not reveal your plans to others too soon.

Whale　　　　　*(inspiration)*
Blessings of spirit are coming. Creative inspiration surrounds you. Act upon it. Dive deep and sing forth your creativity.

Wolf　　　　　*(guidance)*
Though not apparent yet, change is occurring. Trust in self to find your path. Take control. Protection surrounds you in journeys.

Wolverine　　　　　*(persist)*
Persist and do not surrender. This is not a time to surrender. Become ferocious if necessary to overcome troubles.

Zebra　　　　　*(agility brings success)*
Agility – not strength – will bring success now. Do not confront unless there is no other choice. Work around problems and obstacles.

Mammal Notes

Mammal Notes

Chapter Five

Reptiles & Amphibians

Reptiles and amphibians are some of the most ancient creatures on this planet. They are cold-blooded creatures, affected by whatever the temperature of the environment is. Their appearance often tells us of our sensitivity to the world around us and our ability to adapt. Amphibians live in two worlds – part of their life on land and part in water. They reflect our ability to blend worlds and realms – physical and spiritual, male and female, waking and sleeping, etc. Reptiles and amphibians teach us to be selective about what environments we expose ourselves to.

Alligator   *(initiation)*
Act on opportunities for new birth or new knowledge. Initiation is at hand with opportunity for rapid growth.

Basilisk *(dragon)*

Dragon guardianship is about you. New realms will open. Protect your creations but control your emotions. Do not overreact.

Boa Constrictor *(new foundation)*

Hold tight to what is yours. Be true to yourself. Shed what no longer suits you. New foundation is at hand when you build upon yourself.

Box Turtle *(patience)*

Do not rush. You will move through pressures. Let events take their own course. Be patient and do not rush or force.

Chameleon *(opportunity)*

Take advantage of any opportunity that presents itself. Clairvoyance is strong. Act quickly or opportunity will be lost.

Cobra *(swift response)*

Make swift and sudden decisions. Do not be distracted by others. Guard endeavors until ready to act then act quickly.

Copperhead *(aggressive healing)*

Do not give in. Assert changes and look to stronger healing methods. A change in the chemistry of your life of your body is at hand.

Corn Snake   *(climb)*
Easier movement is at hand. You will climb through the past more easily. Take advantage of opportunities for a new path.

Cottonmouth   *(underworld)*
Spiritual initiation is at hand; face your fears. Have faith in strange environments. Guidance and guardianship will be coming.

Crocodile   *(trust in self)*
Only your efforts, strengths and creativity will bring balance. New birth is near. Trust your own instincts and do what is right for you.

Frog   *(fertility)*
Initiate new starts. Explore and accept invitations and offers. Solitary efforts will be more productive.

Garter Snake   *(act)*
Act on as many ideas as possible but do not become overstressed. This is not the time to sit on ideas. Inspiration flows.

Gecko   *(take action)*
Do what must be done in struggles and to handle pests. Express righteous anger is necessary. Bring home conflicts to an end.

Reptiles & Amphibians

Gila Monster *(maintain control)*

Maintain control in all situations. Protect possessions and trust in your beliefs. Do not overextend yourself now.

Green Anole *(harmony)*

Harmony and peace are near. Trust own perceptions – not those of others. Your efforts will pay off with a new foundation.

Horned Toad (Lizard) *(sensitivity)*

You are becoming increasingly sensitive. Express your emotions appropriately. Let others know how you feel.

Iguana *(simplify)*

Break things down and simplify your life. Do not be afraid to climb for new goals. Eliminate what is no longer beneficial for you.

Komodo Dragon *(survival instincts)*

Trust in your survival instincts and perceptions. Do not allow disputes to hinder your efforts. Trust instincts to initiate lasting changes.

Lizard *(subtle perceptions)*

Pay attention to dreams and psychic perceptions. Do not be afraid to detach from problems. Separate and do what you must.

Milk Snake   *(immunity)*

Be more secretive about intentions and activities. Remain immune to the influence of others. Do not let others know weaknesses.

Newt   *(artistic)*

Creative inspirations, ideas & endeavors are strong right now. Do not ignore ideas. Prepare and express your artistic side for success.

Painted Turtle   *(efforts rewarded)*

Have faith. Your efforts and faith are about to be rewarded. Do not stop what you have set in motion. Follow through.

Python   *(faith)*

Be patient. You may need to incubate your ideas a bit more. Put in the necessary work. Faith and persistence is the key to success now.

Rat Snake   *(movement)*

Acceleration and movement comes in all affairs. Don't trust what you see, but what you feel. Assert your efforts now.

Rattlesnake   *(healing)*

Healing and transformation are at hand. Eliminate anything toxic in your life. Opportunities to heal your life grow.

Reptiles & Amphibians

Salamander *(assistance)*

Psychic sensitivity is strong. Pay attention to changes felt. Assistance comes from unexpected sources. Cooperation is critical.

Sea Turtle *(persevere)*

Persevere and great success will come. Senses are heightened so trust in your pursuits. The worst is over; continue forward.

Skink *(hidden found)*

Dig beneath the surface. Hidden things going on around you can be uncovered more easily. In winter, delay digging and exploring.

Snake *(rebirth)*

(See individual species.) Shed the old; new birth is coming. Face fears and do not resist changes. Resurrect some part of your life.

Snapping Turtle *(wariness)*

Handle others with care. Approach new activities with wariness. Be careful of your words being too strong.

Tadpole *(fertility)*

Change is coming. Opportunities for new birth and abundance are at hand. Do not rush things now. Metamorphosis is coming.

Toad   *(inner strength)*

Use the skills and resources available to you. The advantage is yours in conflicts. Don't give into fear. Trust your own resources.

Tortoise   *(move through pressure)*

Pressures are easing and movement is slow but steady. Things will happen in the time and manner best for you. Focus on essentials.

Tuatara   *(slow down)*

Slow down. Be patient until the time is right. Do not allow yourself to be rushed. Delays will be for the best. Work at your own speed.

Turtle   *(promise)*

(See individual species.) Take your time in your pursuits. Trust in Mother Earth. You will have what you need.

Reptile & Amphibian Notes

Chapter Six

Sea Life

Sea/Aquatic life links us to the reality of the dream life – sleeping or waking. Water is a symbol of the astral plane experience, much of which reflects itself in our dreams. Water totems return us to our origins. Fish and other forms of aquatic life make dynamic totems. In ancient myths, tales and religious teachings they often symbolize guidance from our intuitive aspects. Sea life commonly represents independence, potential and possibilities, but only a study of the particular species will truly help us understand its meaning and significance.

Angelfish *(guardian angel)*
Angels are present. Unexpected assistance and opportunity for guardianship are at hand. Give and receive help when you can.

Barracuda   *(go own way)*

It is time to go your own way. Follow your own path. Step out and do not follow the group. Do what you need with little fanfare.

Bass   *(balance opposites)*

Balance opposites and extremes. Face opposition and do not ignore intuition. Be as fertile and creative as possible now.

Carp   *(blessed love)*

Opportunities for achievement are on the horizon – especially in love & relationships. Do not ignore what is essential.

Catfish   *(power of words)*

Your words have great impact now so be discerning about what you say and how you say it. Temper your speech.

Clam   *(relationships)*

Examine relationship(s). Sexual energies and seduction are strong. Be open and truthful to those you are linked.

Coral   *(protection of family)*

Protection surrounds family and creative projects now. Do not hesitate to act on ideas. Your family (work or personal) will expand.

Crab   *(sensitivity)*

Examine issues of sensitivity and reclusiveness. Do not be overprotective of emotions. Trust must be earned.

Crayfish   *(face fears)*

Don't hide from your fears. Now is the time to try to get things done. Do not hide your abilities from others. You are protected.

Damselfish   *(defense)*

Show no fear and defend what is yours. Now is the time to be active and do not let others bully or become aggressive.

Eel   *(new journeys possible)*

Spiritual journey of transformation is ahead. Act on opportunities to explore new depths. Now is time to travel and seek mysteries.

Electric Eel   *(perceptions)*

Trust your own perceptions when life is murky. Things will work out. Do not hesitate to defend yourself or old patterns will continue.

Goldfish   *(peace)*

Peace and prosperity are at hand. Attend to subtle movements and respond accordingly in all things. Focus on your sense of peace.

Grouper *(disguise)*
Disguise what you are doing and feeling to accomplish tasks. Act upon curiosities but do so cautiously. Do rush into things blindly.

Jellyfish *(cooperation)*
Coordinate your work efforts with others. Do not try and do everything yourself. Organization and cooperation insures success.

Moray Eel *(observe)*
Take time to observe from a safe position. Wait for clear opportunity to act. Do not expose yourself or your ideas too openly.

Mussel *(persevere)*
Persevere with endeavors you are attached to. Attach yourself to new opportunities strongly. Sustained efforts will be rewarded.

Octopus *(use intellect)*
Use your intelligence, stealth & camouflage to succeed. Do not act without thinking but be sure to act on your ideas before others do.

Salmon *(persistence)*
A great pilgrimage is ahead. Trust in your feelings for subtle changes. Persistence brings success. Your life is changing so do not give up.

Sea Anemone   *(new tides)*
New tides of wonder are coming. Go slowly as not all is as it seems. New and unusual relationships and realms are coming.

Sea Shell   *(feminine power)*
There is coming a sounding forth of new life, like the trumpeting on a conch shell. Prepare for journeys to a new and protected life.

Sea Horse   *(chivalry)*
Look for dynamic but short period of creativity and romance. Act with chivalrous behavior and do not neglect responsibilities at home.

Shark   *(relentless)*
Senses are heightened. Use relentless ferocity in pursuits/defense of your opportunities. Do not trust the instincts of others. Discriminate.

Squid   *(shapeshifting)*
Pay attention to body language of others rather than their words now. Your ability to read the moods of others is quite accurate. Trust it.

Starfish   *(follow own path)*
Follow your own unique path. Do what is right for you no matter how difficult. It will bring stars of rewards and possibilities.

Stingray *(stay on course)*

Trust in your own inner guidance. You will find what is beneath the surface. Stay on course and trust your inner guidance. Do not hesitate to act.

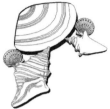

Sea Life Notes

Sea Life Notes

Chapter Seven

Deepening Your Understanding

Determining the significance of your animal encounters is sometimes difficult. This pocket guide will give you a starting point, but it is only that. It is meant to give you initial guidance wherever you go - *because sometimes an animal's message is too important to wait until we get home to explore it.*

Further study though is necessary to determine the full significance of the animal messenger to you and your life. My suggestion is to study much more extensive explanations of the animal's meaning when you have the opportunity in my books *Animal-Speak*, *Animal-Wise* and *Nature-Speak*. And then do research beyond that as well.

Deepening Your Understanding

Is the animal just part of our normal environment? Or does it have a more direct message for us? And if it does, how do we interpret the meaning of animals within our lives? This is not always easy to determine.

Sometimes it will be obvious what the animal means. That skunk that has shown up may not have to do with boundaries at all. It may simply mean it's time to take a bath. Start with the obvious and then more to the more intricate.

Other times it will require some effort to determine the meaning of the animal. Most animals that show up will apply to our life on more than a superficial level. They are frequently multidimensional, reflecting things going on in our life on several levels. By studying the animal and its qualities in relation to people and issues in our life, we begin the process of determining its significance Begin by asking four significant questions and then proceed to the more in-depth exploration of the meaning:

- When we have the encounter with the animal, examine what we were focused upon at that time. What were we doing and/or thinking about at that time? What was most on our mind?

- What have we been most focused upon in the couple hours prior to the encounter? In the previous 24 hours?

- What major issue(s) have been occurring within our life?

- Are there new things you are starting? Have you already or are you about to take up some new endeavors or activities?

Deepening Your Understanding
In-Depth Guide

When we have significant encounters, it is because that animal has something to teach us. It has shown up in our life to show us how to accomplish a task, resolve a problem or remind us of what we are capable. Learning to interpret the message effectively will save us a lot of frustration in our endeavors.

1. Study the species of the animal.

All species of animals of the same type have qualities in common. All reptiles share common, as do mammals, birds, insects, arachnids, and amphibians. These qualities speak generally to you about something going on in your life or something you should be doing.

2. Determine if it is predator or prey.

Most animals in the wild are both predators and prey. Some are distinctly one or the other. Some are more aggressive, some more passive. Some stand their ground when threatened and some move to avoid threats. How does the animal you have encountered handle threats, surprises and the presence of other animals around it? Examining this will help you to determine how assertive and aggressive you should be in handling situations going on around you.

3. Examine the animal specifically.

Every individual animal has unique qualities and characteristics that set it apart from the rest of its species. That animal has appeared in your life because it has qualities specifically beneficial for you and what is going on in your life. Study specifically the following three keys:

Biological Rhythm

Every animal has its own unique life rhythm, times when it is more active, aggressive, procreative, etc. It has a rhythm that enables it to survive more successfully. Some animals hibernate and some are active year round. Some are active at night and some are active during the day. This animal has appeared in your life to tell you that this rhythm is at play within your life.

When we place our own individual schedule into that of the animal (as best we can), we are aligning ourselves with the universal rhythm at play in our life. This saves you a lot of frustration and will help you estimate timelines for accomplishing tasks more successfully.

Adaptive Behaviors

Every animal adapts to survive more successfully. These can be such things as camouflage, remaining still, playing dead, and never following the same path twice and other behaviors. This animal has shown up in your life to tell you that its adaptive behaviors will work best for you right now. Use them.

Crows, for example, will gather and mob birds of prey that come into their territory - especially owls. If they do not drive the owl away, it will come back at night when they can't defend themselves. This mobbing is an adaptive behavior. If you have crows showing up in your life and you have problems or even threats, don't try and handle them yourself. Do what the crow does, get some help and gang up on the problem.

Unique Characteristics

Every animal has unique qualities. Some animals rely on eyesight, some on hearing. Some animals develop natural strength and power, while others develop stalking skills. Some learn to put on displays to attract, distract, romance and alarm. This animal has appeared in your life to tell you to be true to these characteristics and use them for your own greatest success at this time.

For example, a hawk that misses capturing a rabbit does not pretend it's a weasel and chase it on foot. It must learn to fly faster, strike harder and hold tighter. It is true to its unique abilities. If hawk has shown up in your life, success is much more likely if you spot, strike and grasp the opportunities when they present themselves.

4. Examine what's happening in your life.

Look for issues, problems, new activities that you are involved in at the time of the encounter. Are you undertaking new tasks, making changes or moves, trying to solve conflicts and problems?

5. Apply the animal's qualities to what is happening in your life.

This takes practice. It involves analysis, reflection, intuition, some trial and error and even some testing as to whether it truly applies. Start with a simple list of the animal's characteristics along side of a list of issues, activities and endeavors currently on-going within your life. You can even use the note pages at the end of each chapter in this pocket guide for this.

Appendix

Frequently Asked Questions

"OK, let's say I step outside and I see a bird. Does this have meaning?"

Yes, it does have meaning. All animal encounters have significance. Not all of them are direct messages to us about something in our life, but they do have meaning. Sometimes it is just environmental. It is a reminder of the beauty surrounding you. It is telling you to take time to smell the roses. Pay attention to the wonders.

"How do I tell if the animal is personal messenger or just a general environmental message?

There are two kinds of animal encounters: *ordinary* and the *extraordinary*. Seeing a bird as you step out the front door may be an ordinary environmental message, just a reminder of the wonders of Nature. But seeing that bird fly right in front of you and land on your car may be a bit more extraordinary. Unusual behaviors and

Frequently Asked Questions

encounters make it extraordinary and are a more personal message.

Experience is the key, and sometimes it is just developing that "inner knowing". There are two tangible signals that can help you. *First, look for unusual and out-of –the-ordinary behaviors.* For example, seeing an owl is very rare. They are nocturnal and they are very well camouflaged. Hearing an owl is a much more common experience. To see an owl then is a real good indicator that it has a message for you. If you see an owl in the daytime, you are getting what I call a "clue-by-four" up the side of your head. You're getting thumped with its importance.

Secondly, if the animal is a personal message bringer, you will have a variety of encounters with it, all within a relatively short time frame. If the animal is significant for you, it will make its presence known to you in different ways and on more than one occasion. If we dream of the animal and then see it on TV, in stores and in other ways all within a few days, then this animal has a message for us.

"So what are some of the other ways we can encounter animal messengers?"

If we dream of an animal it is the same as meeting it face-to-face in the waking. It should be treated just as significantly. It might come to you in a meditation. Maybe every time you turn on the TV, there is a program on that particular animal. You open a magazine and there are photos of it. You see images of it on billboards, posters and it seems as if you see it every where you turn. When you have several of these within a close time frame, you should pay attention. The animal's archetype and energy is manifesting in your life.

"What does it mean if the animal is poisonous?"

Many animals in the wild are venomous and toxic. Most of these are found in the insect and reptile kingdoms. When there is an encounter with an animal that has some toxicity to it, there are usually issues at hand. Your own body chemistry may be changing. This may be due to healing that is necessary or through natural changes that occur periodically within our life. Adolescence and menopause are two common times when venomous or toxic animals show up as messengers and guides.

Sometimes the meaning of these encounters with animals that have a natural poison to them is more symbolic. It may reflect that the chemistry of your life is changing. It may be telling you about the changes in relationships with family and friends or about jobs and activities that are no longer beneficial to you.

Frequently Asked Questions

"I keep seeing road kill. Does this mean that animal's qualities are dying in me?"

Unfortunately, we live in a time and a place where the natural world intersects with the human world. And sometimes there are causalities resulting from these intersections. It does not mean that the animal's qualities are dying within you. If you notice an animal alongside the road, it has a message for you. Examine what was on your mind at the time you noticed the animal. Sometimes, the noticing is to help the spirit of the animal move on. Say a quiet prayer. It honors the animal and helps keep sacred your bond with Nature.

"Animals keep coming into my backyard and dying. What does that mean?

Although it is sad when such things occur, it is a special honoring of you. Injured and sick animals are very good at camouflaging weaknesses. Most show no signs at all of their condition until it is too late. In the wild any display of weakness, opens them to predation. They have found in your environment that safe place to die – a sanctuary. They have honored you by coming to you at this most vulnerable time. Acknowledge it and honor their passing.

Bibliography

Andrews, Ted. *Animal-Speak*. St. Paul, MN: Llewellyn Publications, 1993.

_____. *Animal-Wise*. Jackson, TN: Dragonhawk Publishing, 1999.

_____. *The Animal-Speak Workbook*. Jackson, TN: Dragonhawk Publishing, 2002.

_____ . *Feathered Omens*. Jackson, TN: Dragonhawk Publishing, 2009.

_____ . *Nature-Speak*. Jackson, TN: Dragonhawk Publishing, 2004.

_____ . *Nature-Speak Oracle*. Jackson, TN: Dragonhawk Publishing, 2006.

_____ . *The Intercession of Spirits*. Jackson, TN: Dragonhawk Publishing, 2008.